George Newman Bliss

The First Rhode Island Cavalry at Middleburg

George Newman Bliss

The First Rhode Island Cavalry at Middleburg

ISBN/EAN: 9783337379896

Printed in Europe, USA, Canada, Australia, Japan

Cover: Foto ©ninafisch / pixelio.de

More available books at **www.hansebooks.com**

THE

FIRST RHODE ISLAND CAVALRY

AT

MIDDLEBURG, VA ,

JUNE 17 AND 18, 1863.

BY

GEORGE N. BLISS,

[Late Captain Troop C, First Rhode Island Cavalry.]

PROVIDENCE:
PUBLISHED BY THE SOCIETY.
1889.

THE FIRST RHODE ISLAND CAVALRY

MIDDLEBURG, VA.

AT the request of many of my comrades I write this paper to correct the errors of other Northern writers upon the events of these two days.

In *the Campaigns of Stuart's Cavalry*, by Major H. B. McClellan, pages 303, 304 and 305, the deeds of the First Rhode Island Cavalry at this time are set forth in words as accurate as they are complimentary, but this gallant Confederate officer cannot afford the space for details as embraced in the work of our Society.

The following extracts contain some errors of Northern historians :

History of the Civil War in America, Compte De Paris, Vol. III., page 494 :

It is the movement of Colonel Duffié by way of Thoroughfare Gap, which was accomplished in the midst of the greatest dangers and with wonderful daring, but also with heavy loss, which finally led to the retreat of Munford. Duffié, with his two hundred and eighty men, had unexpectedly made his appearance in front of Chambliss' brigade, but he had succeeded in disguising his numerical weakness from the Confederates, who were entirely worn out, and little desirous, undoubtedly, to bring on an action ; so that while Chambliss was under the impression that he had a superior force to deal with, Duffié, stealing away in the night, was rapidly marching upon Middleburg.

Chancellorsville and Gettysburg by Doubleday, page 102 :

Colonel Duffié's division started from Centreville for Middleburg, by way of Thoroughfare Gap, but finding the enemy (W. H. F. Lee's brigade) were already in the Gap, they went around through Hopewell Gap and kept on to Middleburg, which Duffié reached about 9.30 A. M.

The battle of Bunker Hill was upon the 17th and that of Waterloo on the 18th of June. It was the fortune of the First Rhode Island Cavalry to be in action upon both anniversaries in the year 1863, and the history of the regiment for these two days is one of disaster, but not of dishonor.

Early in the morning of June 17, 1863, the following order was received :

Col. A. N. Duffié First Rhode Island Cavalry:

You will proceed with your regiment from Manassas Junction by the way of Thoroughfare Gap, to Middleburg; there you will camp for the night, and communicate with the headquarters of the Second Cavalry Brigade. From Middleburg you will proceed to Union ; thence to Snickersville; from Snickersville to Percyville ; thence to Wheatland, and, passing through Waterford, to Nolan's Ferry, where you will join your brigade.

The day was bright with sunshine, and the regiment, numbering two hundred and eighty sabres, took the road without a thought of the future. At Thoroughfare Gap privates Duxbury, Lee and Teft, of Company H, were in the advance; Duxbury meets a Confederate cavalry picket, and fires his carbine but misses his enemy, at that time on a full gallop in retreat. A few shots came from the woods, but our skirmishers soon drove the pickets back upon a larger force. "There are six hundred of them, I think," said Duxbury to Captain Chase ; "There are at least twice as many as there are of us." In the skirmish three of our horses were killed and several horses were wounded, but none of the troopers were hit. Having passed through the Gap and reached the desired road, Duffié turned to the right and pressed forward towards Middleburg, some fifteen miles away. In thus obeying orders, Duffié left behind him W. H. F. Lee's brigade, under command of Col. J. R. Chambliss, estimated as twelve hundred men, while at Aldie Gap, fifteen miles further north in the mountain range, now enclosing the Rhode Island troops on the east, Fitz Lee's Brigade consisting of the First, Second, Third, Fourth and Fifth Virginia, were that day to hold their position against our entire cavalry corps under command of General Pleasanton. General Robertson's brigade, ten thousand strong, was at Rector's Cross Roads, eight miles west of Middleburg, in which town General Stuart, commanding these three Confederate brigades of cavalry, was enjoying the hospitality of his friends, protected only by a body guard of three companies. At 4 p. m. the First Rhode Island struck Stuart's pickets, and at once charged them, driving Stuart and his staff out of Middleburg on the gallop, escaping capture only by reason of the superior speed of their fresh horses. At this time Fitz Lee's brigade had been engaged at Aldie, only five miles away, for two hours with Kilpatrick's troopers, holding the Gap against charge after charge of our brave cavalrymen.

General Stuart thought the force that had penetrated to the very centre of his troopers must be a large one, and at once sent orders to Robertson's, Fitz Lee's, and W. H. F. Lee's brigades to concentrate upon Middleburg. Duffié has obeyed orders; he is in Middleburg where he is ordered to remain for the night; he does not know that at Aldie, five miles in his rear, Colonel Munford, commanding Fitz Lee's Brigade, is holding our whole Cavalry Corps at bay. A movement of the First Rhode Island on Aldie would have struck the Confederate rear and changed defeat to victory, but this is imagination, not history, and in accordance with our orders Capt. Frank Allen, with two men, was sent to Aldie with a dispatch for Pleasanton, and I know of no better description of his ride then the following official report:

CAMP FIRST RHODE ISLAND CAVALRY,
ALEXANDEIA, VA.
June 22, 1863.

Col. A. N. Duffié:

SIR: I have the honor to report, that about five o'clock, P. M., on the evening of the 17th instant, I was sent from Middleburg, where the regiment was then engaged with the enemy, to carry a dispatch to General Kilpatrick at Aldie, accompanied by two men. I first attempted to proceed by the main road, but was halted and fired upon by a body of the enemy, who said they were the Fourth Virginia Cavalry. I then returned towards Middleburg, and leaving the road attempted to make my way across the country. I found the fields and woods in every direction full of bodies of the enemy; by exercising the greatest care, I succeeded in making my way through them to Little River. Here I encountered five of the enemy, and forced them to give me passage. Following the river down, I struck the main road about one mile from Aldie, and by inquiry learned that our pickets were on that road.

I reached Aldie and delivered my dispatch to General Kilpatrick at 9 P. M. General Kilpatrick informed me that his brigade was so worn out that he could not send any reinforcements to Middleburg, but that he would report the situation of our regiment to General Gregg. Returning, he said that General Gregg had gone to state the facts to General Pleasanton, and directed me to remain at Aldie until he heard from General Pleasanton. I remained, but received no further orders.

Respectfully submitted,

FRANK ALLEN,

Captain First Rhode Island Cavalry.

Colonel Duffié posted strong pickets at barricades across the roads leading out of Middleburg on the south, west and north, and stationed his reserve on the road leading towards Aldie at the east of the town. For three hours the regiment held undisputed possession of the place, but at seven o'clock in the evening General Stuart returned with the Fourth and Fifth North Carolina Cavalry, about one thousand strong; the men at the barricades fought bravely but were soon outflanked and driven back upon the reserve. Warned by the attack on the outposts, Colonel Duffié ordered companies G and F, numbering about sixty, to dismount, tie their horses to trees in the grove, which at that time sheltered and concealed the regiment, and form a line behind a stone wall that bounded one side of the road. By this time it was quite dark, and as the enemy charged towards us in column, the first notice they had of the ambuscade was the discharge of sixty carbines, when four rebels were abreast of each gun. Horses and men fell in confusion, and the rebels retreated in disorder under a hot fire from the revolvers of the men who had just emptied their carbines. The rebel officers could be heard rallying their men for another charge, which was soon made and as soon repulsed. Again their officers were heard saying, "Now, boys, form once more; we'll give 'em h—l this time; we will sweep every Yankee from the face of the earth," and a third time they charged and were again hurled back shattered and torn. While this fighting was in progress I was with the remaining men of the regiment, mounted and facing the enemy in the woods, a few yards from the left of our line of dismounted men ready to charge on any force that might pass the ambuscade. After the last charge it was evident that the rebels had learned something, and they commenced to form a line out-flanking the road instead of trying another charge in column along the road. Maj. P M. Farrington sent Lieut. J. M. Fales to report to Colonel Duffié that the enemy were about to deploy in the fields and attack his right flank and rear, and to ask for orders. Lieutenant Fales found that the regiment had moved, and followed the retiring column two miles before overtaking Duffié, and the Colonel said to him, " Stay with the regiment ; it is of no use to go back, you will be captured." It is claimed that Colonel Duffié sent orders to Major Farrington to fall back from the wall, mount and join the regiment, but that in the darkness and confusion somebody blundered, and the brave men who had thrice repulsed the enemy were left to meet their fate alone. Major

Farrington mounted his men after he had heard the rebel officers give the order " Cease firing, dismount and go into those woods," and attempted to join the regiment ; but at this time a mounted force of rebel cavalry had entered the woods, and Captain Chase, after joining his men to a Confederate column, supposing it to be the First Rhode Island Cavalry, did not discover his mistake until called upon to surrender. Warned by the loud summons for surrender given to Captain Chase, Major Farrington with two officers and twenty-three men moved off a short distance into the woods, where they dismounted and remained concealed twenty-four hours within gun-shot of large forces of the rebels until the advance of our cavalry corps from Aldie gave them the opportunity to rejoin the Union troops.

Colonel Duffié, with what remained of the regiment, numbering now less than two hundred, retreated at a walk a little over two miles, and went into camp in the woods, where we halted under arms without unsaddling horses until daybreak. By this time there was no soldier so dull as not to understand the desperate situation of the regiment.

2

We had left behind us at Thoroughfare Gap a force of the enemy larger than our own. At Middleburg we had learned that a large force of the enemy had passed through that day going towards Aldie and we were only two miles distant, at most, from the hostile force five times our number in strength and by which we had been driven from the town we had been ordered to hold. With the Bull Run Mountains on the east and the Confederates in our front at every other point in the compass, we were hiding in the woods, knowing that the rising sun would betray us to an overwhelming force of the enemy moving upon us from all directions. No fires were allowed and no talking was permitted except in so low a tone of voice as to amount to whispering, but the thought was universal and freely expressed that our only hope was to move at once and charge through the enemy's lines in the night. Had any native born officer been in command the regiment would, without doubt, have cut its way out that night and could not have met in so doing greater disaster than was to befall it on the morrow. Colonel Duffié was a Frenchman, he had received positive orders and thought it his duty to obey them. In a letter written afterwards he says, "I could certainly have saved my regiment in the night, but my duty as a soldier and as Colonel obliged me to be faithful to my orders. During those moments of reflection, and knowing that my regiment was being sacrificed, contemplating all this through more than five hours, my heart was bleeding in seeing the lives of those men, whom I had led so many times, sacrificed through the neglect and utter forgetfulness of my superior officers ; but in the midst of my grief I found some consolation, beholding the manner in which the Rhode Island boys fought."

Just before day I received orders from Colonel Duffié to go on foot outside the woods in the direction of the road to Thorougfare Gap and see if I could discover any signs of the enemy. I obeyed the order and remained in the open fields until the increasing light of the opening day gave me an opportunity to see the road for some distance, but saw nothing of the enemy and so reported to Colonel Duffié. My report was hardly made before shots from the enemy were heard fired upon our pickets

facing towards Middleburg. The regiment was at
once ordered to mount and we moved out into the
road in column of fours, my company was at the
head of the regiment facing towards the south on
the same road I had shortly before been scouting
on foot. As we were then with our backs towards
the enemy that had fired upon our pickets, the order
was given "Fours right about," I had given the first
part of the order, " Fours right about," and was on
the point of finishing it with "March!" when I discovered a force of rebel cavalry charging upon us
not more than seventy-five yards away. Pointing
my sabre towards the enemy I at once gave the
order to charge, and just at that moment the rebel
officer leading the charge leveled his pistol and fired
at me with so good an aim that the bullet struck
my sabre blade, and glancing, drew blood on my
right arm, the sensation being as though my arm
had been struck smartly with a whip. At that
moment I saw that Colonel Duffié was on the oppo-
site side of the first set of fours, and he said, "Go
ahead boys, charge!" but his tone and manner was
that of one having no hope of success. The men

wavered, broke, and jumped their horses over a
a stone wall into a wheat-field on the east side of
the road, and, through the waving wheat, the regiment rushed in confusion with the rebels close after
them. We had passed through the wheat-field and
by the farmer's house, who, reckless of danger, and
without thought of the flying bullets, stood on his
piazza cursing the soldiers as their horses trampled
under foot his lusty grain, when I heard an order
from Colonel Thompson, " Captain Bliss, halt ! rally
the men. We have gone far enough." This order
I obeyed at once, and found it hard at first to get
the men to stop their retreat, and face the enemy,
but as soon as I had six men in line facing the rebels
the rest of the regiment came into line of battle
like the snapping of a whip. The rebels were
stopped by this move and opened fire upon us with
carbines, and they were so near that when the Confederate officer said to his men, " Let's give them a
sabre charge," every soldier of the First Rhode Island heard it, and when I shouted back in defiance,
" That is just what we want," there were loud de-
mands in our ranks of " Let us charge." The order

to charge was given at once and we had the pleasure
of seeing the same men that had charged us running
away through the same wheat field, and of feeling
that our disgrace was in some measure removed.
We were halted in the wheat-field, where a line of
battle was formed, and we counted off by fours in
each rank. The rebels we had driven retreated in
the direction from which our pickets had been fired
upon a short time before. Lieut. James M. Fales,
who was captured while we were retreating through
this same field, says, in his Prison Life, No. 15,
second series, page 9 : "After going about an eighth
of a mile from the wheat-field, where I was captured, I saw a force of about five thousand rebel
cavalry, and thought that my regiment, on that
morning, not more than two hundred strong, would
be annihilated, and to this day it seems wonderful
to me that so many as one hundred succeeded in
cutting their way into the Union lines."

Colonel Duffié was fully aware of our desperate
situation ; he ordered the regiment into column of
fours and said to me, " Captain Bliss, you will take
the head of the column, no obstacle whatever stop

you, we are surrounded here ; we must cut our way
out." We took the road towards Hopeville Gap,
the same road over which a few minutes before Captain Haynes had charged upon us at the head of
companies G and H of the Ninth Virginia Cavalry,
and moved on at a walk, the usual marching gait.
We had marched less than a mile when I heard
shots in the rear, and soon Colonel Duffié came gal-
loping to the head of the column and said, " Cavalry
in our rear, boys. Let us go," and we went. The
horse I brought from Rhode Island, and which had
carried me so many miles, had been lost on the 16th
of June at Mannassas by carelessness and disobedi-
ence of orders by my negro servant in letting the
animal graze without a picket rope, and I was rid-
ing a horse loaned me by Lieutenant Vaughan, and
sitting an English instead of a military saddle. The
ride was after the style of let the best horse win,
and frequently my feet would be thrown out of my
light stirrups by crowding horses in the narrow road
which caused me to slacken the pace while regaining
the stirrups, and so it soon happened that although
I started at the head of the procession I found my-

sely rapidly falling back towards the rear. At last I was where I could hear the rebels shouting, "Surrender, its no use, you can't get away," and hear their bullets sing as they fired into the column, and could also see our men turning in their saddles and firing back through the dust that covered us all like a heavy fog. I saw that if I continued in the road I must soon be killed, or taken prisoner, and noticing that on the mountain side of the road there was no fence I reined my horse sharply to the left, but he was determined to follow the column and did not obey the rein. For a moment I thought I was lost, but, with a desperate effort, I gave him the rein again together with my left spur, and making a slight angle with the road he darted into the woods at a point where there was a tree with limbs so low as to sweep me over the horse's tail and leave me sitting on the ground with a drawn sabre in my right hand, while the horse rapidly disappeared forever from my sight among the thick woods of the mountain side. As I sat there I saw that several of my comrades had followed my lead, and they passed by me into the woods. Although but a few yards from the road the air was so thick with dust that the whole rebel column thundered by without a man discovering me, and as soon as they had passed I rose and climbed up the mountain a short distance, where I found six men of my regiment in a dense thicket of laurel bushes within a short gun-shot of the road. I sat down among them to rest, and as I always carried with me a pocket inkstand and writing materials, I improved the time by writing to my old college chum, David V. Gerald, the following letter :

NEAR BULL RUN MTS., VA.,

June 18, 1863.

Our regiment has just been cleaned up. We left Manassas Junction yesterday morning. We had a skirmish at Thoroughfare Gap, but succeeded in forcing a passage with a loss of only three horses killed and some wounded. We reached Middleburg, having had considerable skirmishing along the road. We found a small party of rebel cavalry in this place, but drove them out and established our pickets, expecting hourly the rest of our brigade to join us, via. Aldie, but it seems General Stuart, with a large force, had already taken Aldie and so we were left out in the cold, or rather shut up in among the mountains, in a regular trap, entirely surrounded by the rebels. Just after sunset last night the rebel cavalry charged upon us with overwhelming numbers. Our men fought stubbornly, and many rebs bit the dust, but it was no use, we were obliged to retreat, which we did in good order, leaving about eighty of our men killed, wounded and prisoners; we fell back about two miles and stopped. We had no guides, and did not know in what direction to go. At daybreak the enemy attacked us and we retreated. By this time the men were very much discouraged, knowing our hopeless condition. We had gone but a short distance when we were attacked, both in front and in rear. Our plain duty was to charge and cut our way through, but the men would not do it. At this time, while at the head of the column, trying to get the men to charge with me, a bullet struck the blade of my sabre and glancing wounded me slightly in the right fore arm, but it is only a scratch, does not interfere, as you see, with writing. The men went into a field to the left of the road, and ran promiscuously. At last, by tremendous exertion on the part of the officers, the men were rallied, and we charged the rebels, who ran when they saw we meant fight. We then continued our retreat, but the rebels came down on our rear before we had gone a mile, and routed our men completely. I was at the head of the column, and had orders to charge and cut my way through all obstructions, and I did not believe anything short of artillery or a barricade would have stopped us, but the attack on the rear was fatal. Colonel Duffié rode by me saying, " Cavalry in our rear, boys, let us go," and we *did go*. I traveled with the rest about three miles, and the rebels were constantly shooting down men at the rear of the column. I lost my big bay horse several days ago, and found myself gradually dropping to the rear, and saw I must soon be shot or be taken prisoner unless I did something for myself with great swiftness, so I just dashed off sideways into the woods, a tree swept me from the saddle, and I stopped while the horse went on. Some of the men saw my dodge, and imitated the same, and I have six men and five horses here with me. We have been lying here for an hour listening to the rebels talk. They are constantly passing by here, but they will have to be smart to catch this crowd. I intend to pilot this crowd safely out of the woods; but we have got a hard row to hoe among these mountains.

I hear a rebel damning a prisoner. I don't know whether you will ever get this letter; if you don't get it write, and if you do get it write; but by all means write. I suppose nearly all our regiment are either killed, wounded or prisoners by this time; another sacrifice to poor generalship. Still, I think our affairs never looked brighter. If Lee will only go with his army fifty miles into Pennsylvania we shall clean him up. This letter is private. I don't care if Tom Bishop, or any one else you can trust, sees it, but don't care to have the main facts public.

June 19, 1863.

I have been successful in joining the remnant of our regiment. I brought off with me

Edward C. Capwell, Hospital Steward.
William J. Bowley, [M] Troop.
Sergt. Alvin S. Eaton, [M] Troop.
George H. Dix, [M] Troop.
E. Carns, [M] Troop.
James H. Collins, [A] Troop.

Perhaps it may be advisable to publish these names as safe. From talk with various officers, who have escaped, I am sure the rebels suffered severely; in fact, I think their loss equal to ours. About forty of those in the fight have got in.

Lt.-Col. Thompson,	Lt. Ellis,
Capt. Allen,	Capt. Gould,
Lt. Prentiss,	Capt. Bliss,
Lt. Brown,	Lt. Shurtleff.

Of those officers who went out, these are all who have returned up to date, but we have good reason to think that there are more in the mountains who will come in sooner or later.

Publish the names of these officers.

I was obliged to abandon our horses, and make our way over the mountains on foot, but I saved my arms. The bullet that wounded me, struck the blade of my sabre, and glancing scratched my arm. The bullet would undoubtedly have struck my body if it had not glanced from my sabre. I hope to return the compliment with the same sabre before the war is over. Lieutenant Burgess, Captain Rhodes and Lieutenant Vaughan went to Washington sick, June 17th, and were not in the fight. Tell father, Charles was not in the fight and is all right somewhere. When you get this please inform father of my safety immediately. I am obliged to make this one letter answer for all. Daniel W. Ide, of East Providence, was not in the fight, having been with the dismounted men since April 13th.

It is too bad to slaughter a regiment needlessly as we were.

I may be egotistical, but I believe that if I had been in command I would have safely extricated the regiment from its perilous condition on the night of June 17th. I would have gone to a house, taken a man and told him to take me across Bull Run mountains, and that if he brought me among the rebs I would blow out his brains on the spot. We were halted all night when we ought to have been marching. But it is no use to lament the past; let us profit by our sad experience and do better next time. While I can knaw hard bread I shall never say die.

Yours truly,

G. N. BLISS.

After writing the first part of the foregoing letter I assumed command of the party, and we moved towards the summit of the mountain, feeling sure we would find Union troops on the east side, if we could succeed in crossing. Having my field-glass with me I went in advance, and at every opportunity viewed the country I saw the rebel videttes at cross-roads in the distance, and could, therefore, easily avoid them. As we were going along the mountain side we disturbed a partridge with her brood of young, and they ran in front of us for several yards, and nothing I saw in my whole soldier life, awoke in me so strong a longing for home and the pursuits of peaceful life. After traveling some miles we found we were not on the Bull Run Mountain, but on an outlying hill, and must descend into a valley to reach the ridge we wished to cross. In the valley we found a delightful brook of clear cold water, and determined to rest and refresh our horses here. We bathed in the brook, and then seeing an approaching thunder-storm, put up our shelter tents and waited for the shower to pass. Just as the rain was ceasing, two mounted rebels

3

passed near us, and as we saw them it was reasona-
able to suppose they saw us, and to conjecture that a
larger force was near by, from whom we might soon
expect an attack. We determined, therefore, to
abandon our horses and climb the mountain, at a
point where it was too rough for horses to travel.
It was about dark as we pushed on up the mountain
side over rocks and among brush and briars, until,
about ten o'clock, we found a clearing on the mountain top with a house in its centre. After careful re-
connoitering we found only two persons were there,
and then asked admission. The lady of the house was
about sixty years old, and was reluctant to admit us,
but we insisted, and as we had some silver with us,
and paid it for our supper of corn-bread and milk,
she became quite sociable. She had never seen a
Yankee before, but had once possessed a Yankee
needle and a Yankee pin. We put one man on
picket, and the others had a comfortable night lying
before the wood-fire burning in the huge stone fire-
place. In the morning after a breakfast of corn-
bread and milk, we started down the east side of
the mountain, and in a few hours caught sight of a

cavalry picket, and passing through the lines soon found Major Turner and a small squad of our men, who had not been with the regiment on its unfortunate raid. A few days later those who had escaped from this disaster were assembled at Alexandria. Colonel Duffié, with four officers and twenty-seven men, escaped through Hopewell Gap and marched to Centreville, where he made so good a report to General Hooker that he was recommended by him to be promoted and receive a commission as Brigadier-General, dated June 17, 1863. It is reported that General Duffié said, " My goodness, when I do well, they take no notice of me. When I go make one bad business, make one fool of myself, they promote me, make me General."

In all the fighting of the first day we did not have a man wounded ; and if the regiment had cut its way out during the night of the 17th, the affair would have been a brilliant feat of arms, as we had penetrated to the centre of Stuart's Cavalry, and caused him to change all his plans and order Munford to fall back from the strong position where he was at Aldie, holding our entire cavalry force at bay. On the second day, the 18th, we had six killed and twenty wounded; the killed were Lieutenant J A. Chedell (C), Corporal T Burton (F), S. Wilcox (D), J H. Elkins (M), Charles Fairbanks (M), and B. G. Lawrence (M).

We had in the two days 210 captured, but forty of them succeeded in escaping, and only 170 were taken as prisoners to Richmond. The Color-Sergeant, G. A. Robinson (Troop I), when he found he would be captured took the colors from the staff and wrapped them around his body under his clothing, and after being a prisoner for several days escaped, and brought the colors safely back to the regiment, for which he was rewarded by promotion to the rank of Lieutenant. During the confusion of our first retreat through the wheat-field in the morning of June 18th, a rebel rode up to Lawrence Cronan, who carried the guidon of Company C, and demanded the surrender of the flag. Cronan refused, and the rebel fired, sending a bullet through Cronan's right arm, his breast, and wounding his left arm, but Cronan rode off with the flag as though nothing had happened. Soon after, Cronan

became faint through loss of blood, gave his flag to
a comrade, and was left behind a prisoner.   Cronan
was taken to Middleburg, but was recaptured at
noon of the 18th, when our cavalry corps entered
the town, was sent to the hospital at Washington,
recovered from his wounds, and served until the end
of the war.   While Cronan was lying wounded and
a prisoner, the rebel who shot him came to his side
and said, " Why did you not surrender that flag,"
to which Cronan replied, "It was not given me for
that purpose."   The rebel said, " Well, you are
tough," and passed on.

Several of my comrades have, at my request, written out their personal experience in this affair, and
their narratives, and the letters and papers from
Confederate sources published in the appendix to
this paper, renders it unnecessary for me to prolong
my own story.

This movement of the First Rhode Island Cavalry
on Middleburg, resulting in disaster to the regiment, was of great service to our arms.   It at once
resulted in an order from General Stuart for the retreat of his troops from Aldie, where they had held

a position so strong that our whole cavaliy corps had failed to dislodge them. Our cavalry passed the Aldie Gap and for several days pushed Stuart's troops severely, and it is thought that General Stuart's desire to retaliate by a brilliant feat of arms led him to make the raid between Washington and the Army of the Potomac, thereby depriving General Lee of the services of Stuart and his veteran cavalrymen for many days, and for want of the information they might have given, causing, as many Confederate officers believe, the crushing defeat at Gettysburg.

APPENDIX.

LEXINGTON, KY., 1st July, 1884.

Capt. George N. Bliss, Providence, R. I.:

MY DEAR SIR: Your favors of recent date are received. I think I can answer your questions satisfactorily, and you will find that the statements which I shall make are, in the main, verified by Gen. Stuart's report, to which you doubtless have access.

On the morning of the 17th June, '63, Stuart moved Fitz Lee's Brigade, commanded by Col. T. T. Munford, from Piedmont to Aldie. Robertson's Brigade was stationed at Rector's Cross Roads, and W. H. F. Lee's Brigade, commanded by Col. Chambliss, was left near Salem to picket Thoroughfare Gap, and to keep open communication with Hampton, who was still in the rear.

Stuart detached from Fitz Lee's Brigade two squadrons to accompany himself as body guard and for picket duty, and with these two squadrons took station at Middleburg as a central point of communication between his brigades. It was doubtless Stuart's intention to move Chambliss and Robertson towards Middleburg later in the day. When Col. Duffié reached Thoroughfare Gap there was no Confederate force in his front but the picket from Chambliss' command, and this picket was no doubt instructed to report to the brigade headquarters, and was not instructed to report to Stuart at Middleburg. Hence Stuart was not aware of Duffié's advance until it encountered the picket thrown out by his body

guard from Middleburg. The distance from Salem to Thoroughfare Gap is about eight miles, and from Salem to Middleburg, perhaps twice as far; so you will readily see that unless the picket at
the Gap had been instructed to report direct to Stuart, the news
of Duffié's advance could not have reached Stuart in time to pre-
pare him for it. Duffié's movement was certainly a surprise, in the
sense that Stuart had no notice of it, but the (for him) very un-
usual precaution which he had taken of attaching to himself a
strong body guard, showed that he was prepared for unexpected
developments, and although unable to dispute the road with Col.
Duffié, he had sufficient time to notify Munford, at Aldie, of the
danger in his rear, and then to retire in safety from Middleburg.
There is no doubt whatever about the fact that Munford's with-
drawal from the Aldie Gap was caused by the order sent by Stuart,
when he was driven out of Middleburg by Duffié. Munford could,
and would have held his position in spite of all his opponents could
do. One of his best regiments had hardly fired a gun, and another
had been but little hurt. His position was a strong one, and the
fighting, while severe, had only served to warm up his men and
give them confidence. But what else could Stuart do but order
him to retire? Munford was now between two forces, and Stuart
could not count upon the arrival of either Chambliss or Robertson
in time to relieve him. Had Duffié been aware of the state of
affairs at Aldie, and had he moved upon Munford instead of stop-
ping at Middleburg, your regiment would have escaped the disaster which befell it, and might have inflicted serious damage on
Munford.

In my article reviewing the Comte de Paris, I have stated the
loss in the 1st R. I. Regiment, as given by Col. Duffié in his official
report. This report justifies me in asserting the annihilation of
the regiment, for Col. Duffié states the survivors to be " 4 officers

and 27 men." I find no subsequent report contradicting this, or in any way mitigating the disaster to the regiment. Duffié's report was, however, written on the same day on which he reached his brigade, and it seems reasonable that others, of whom he was not at that time aware, might have made their escape and rejoined their friends at a later day. I will be glad if you can give me any exact and *authoritative* information concerning the loss in your regiment. What became of the regimental organization? Was it ever restored, and did the regiment again come into the field? I am anxious, not only to make no error on this point, but also to do full justice to a gallant body of men, who were overwhelmed by a disaster, which was in no sense the result of any fault of their own.

If there are any other points upon which I can give you information, please command me.

I am yours very sincerely,

H. B. McCLELLAN.

LEXINGTON, KY., 10 July, 1884.

Captain Geo. N. Bliss, Providence, R. I. :

MY DEAR SIR: I thank you sincerely for your kind favors of the 5th instant, and for the History of the First Rhode Island Cavalry, which you present to me in the name of your Veteran Association. Please convey to the Association my thanks for this valuable and highly appreciated gift. I shall not fail, now that the facts are before me, to correct some errors into which I have been led by the absence of full reports in the official records.

The force which attacked the 1st Rhode Island Cavalry at Middleburg on the 17th June, 1863, was Robertson's Brigade, which consisted of the 59th North Carolina State Troops (4th Cavalry Regiment), Col. D. D. Ferrebee ; and the 63d North Carolina State

Troops (5th Cavalry), Col. P. G. Evans. These two regiments were fresh from the camp of instruction, and on the 31st May reported about 1,000 aggregate present for duty. They were present, but not engaged at the battle of the 9th June, near Brandy Station. They probably had 900 men in the saddle on the 17th June, but this was the first time they came under fire. They were armed with Enfield rifles and sabres. They were badly cut up in the fights of the 19th and 21st June, but subsequently, under Gordon and Barringer, became veteran regiments and did excellent service. Col. Evans was killed at Upperville, on the 21st June.

I regret that I cannot answer your question concerning the force engaged with your regiment on the 18th July, 1863. Perhaps General Stuart's report on the Gettysburg Campaign may throw some light on that point, see Southern Historical Society papers, Vol. 7, page 428, at the bottom of the page.

I am, dear Sir, yours very sincerely,

H. B. McCLELLAN.

The following extract is from the *Campaigns of Stuart's Cavalry*, by Major H. B. McClellan; pages 303, 304 and 305 :

Early in the morning Col. A. N. Duffié had crossed the Bull Run Mountain at Thoroughfare Gap. His orders directed him to encamp at Middleburg on the night of the 17th, and to proceed the next day towards Nolan's Ferry, extending his march to the west as far as Snickersville. These orders seem to have contemplated a somewhat extended scout by this regiment on the left flank of General Gregg's division,—a hazardous movement in the presence of an enterprising enemy. Col. Duffié reached Thoroughfare Gap at 9.30 A. M., and was somewhat delayed in crossing the mountain by the picket from Chambliss' command. By eleven o'clock, however, he was fairly on his way towards Middleburg. At four o'clock, P. M., he struck the pickets which Stuart had established for his own safety outside the town, and drove them in so quickly that Stuart and his staff were compelled to make a retreat more rapid than was consistent with dignity and comfort. Having with him no force adequate to contest the ground with Duffié's regiment, Stuart retired toward Rector's Cross Roads. Munford was notified of his danger, and directed to withdraw from Aldie, and Robertson and Chambliss were orderd to move immediately upon Middleburg. The only hope for Duffié's regiment now lay in an immediate advance upon Aldie, where he might have created considerable commotion by attacking the rear of the 1st Virginia Cavalry on the Middleburg road. But he did not know this, and his orders were positive, requiring him to encamp for the night at Middleburg. He therefore made the best of his situation by dismounting one-half of his regiment behind stone walls and barricades, hoping that he might be able to hold his position until reinforced from Aldie, whither he sent Captain Frank Allen to make known his situation at brigade headquarters. Captain Allen reached Aldie, after encountering many difficulties, at nine o'clock, P. M. He says in his report, " General Kilpatrick informed me that his brigade was so worn out that he could not send any reinforcements to Middleburg, but that he would report the situation of our regiment to General Gregg. Returning, he said that General Gregg had gone to state the facts to General Pleasanton, and directed me to remain at Aldie until he heard from General Pleasanton. I remained, but received no further orders."

Thus Colonel Duffié was left to meet his fate. At seven o'clock in the evening he was attacked by Robertson's brigade. His men fought bravely, and repelled more than one charge before they were driven from the town, retiring by the same road upon which they had advanced. Unfortunately for Duffié, this road was now closed by Chambliss' brigade, which surrounded him during the night, and captured, early the next morning, the greater part of those who had escaped from Robertson on the previous evening. Colonel Duffié himself, escaped capture, and reached Centreville early in the afternoon, with four of his officers and twenty-seven men. He reports the loss in his regiment at twenty officers and two hundred and forty-eight men. This, however, was an exaggeration of the calamity; for other officers beside himself had taken to the woods, and succeeded in making their way back to the Federal lines on the 18th and 19th. Major Farrington, who was separated from his regiment on the night of the 17th, in Middleburg, thus brought in two officers and twenty-three men; Lieutenant-Colonel Thompson brought in eighteen men; Sergeant Palmer, twelve men; and Captain George N. Bliss, six men. Color-Sergeant Robbins, who was wounded and captured, was left in Middleburg, and fell into the hands of his friends when Stuart retired from that place. This reduces the loss to two hundred. This regiment was composed of good materials, and it rapidly recuperated. On the 17th of August following it assembled three hundred men at Warrenton, and was attached to McIntosh's brigade, of Gregg's division.

LYNCHBURG, VIRGINIA, April 30, 1884.

Major George N. Bliss:

DEAR SIR: Immediately after I received your letter asking me about the fight at Aldie, 17th June, 1863, I addressed the enclosed letter to Capt. Frank S. Robertson, who resides in Washington County, Virginia, thinking he could recall the circumstances connected with the order. His reply is herewith enclosed. Capt. Robertson was A. A. D. C. on Gen'l Stuart's staff,—this should settle the point as to whether *I* was *ordered off or drawn off.* It matters very little to me. *I left* there, and as I had a strong position, would have preferred holding it to having a fight with a largely superior force where I did not and could not have the advantages of the strong position I had taken at Aldie.

I was not *pressed* or harassed to any extent when I did fall back, and I certainly carried off all of my prisoners, and did not leave any of my wounded that could be moved.

I am, Major, very truly and respectfully,

THOMAS T. MUNFORD.

LYNCHBURG, April 22, 1884.

Capt. Frank Robertson, A. A. D. C. late A. N. Va.:

DEAR CAPT.: I enclose you a letter from a gallant Federal officer, Major Geo. N. Bliss, he asked some information at my hands about the battle at Aldie, 17th June, 1864. Remembering that you came in person and delivered an order to me from Gen'l J. E. B. Stuart to fall back from my position at Aldie, will you please state that fact on the other side of the page of this letter. A good many reports have been made on this fight and the Federals claim that we were driven off. I reported that I was ordered by Gen'l Stuart to fall back, through you as his A. D. C. I will thank you to state as far as you can what orders you delivered to me.

Your friend,

THOMAS T. MUNFORD.

If you will do me the kindness to enclose Capt. Frank S. Robertson's letter to Major H. B. McClellan's address, Lexington, Kentucky, after *satisfying* yourself. It will be an introduction to Major

4

McClellan, who will be better able to give you information than I can.

This captain's reply was not received until to-day, and I did not wish to delay my reply to your letter, hence I did not send it in my hurried letter a few days since.

Yours,

T. J. M.

THE MEADOWS IN ABINGDON, VA., April 26, 1884.

Gen'l Thos. T. Munford :

DEAR SIR: In reply to yours will state that the orders I carried you from Gen. J. E. B. Stuart were delivered under difficulties that vividly recall them. He and Staff were very unceremoniously driven out of Middleburg by the sudden and unexpected approach of a large body of Federal Cavalry. Shortly afterwards General Stuart called me and gave the following orders: "Go back and find Munford about Aldie, explain matters, and order him to fall back immediately and join me as best he can at Rector's Cross Roads to night." Less than an hour afterwards these orders were given you at Aldie, and as I remember quite late in the evening.

I found you sharply engaged, but recall no impression of the enemy's pressing or having anything to do with your falling back, which, of course, immediately followed my orders from Stuart.

Yours very truly,

FRANK S. ROBERTSON.

LYNCHBURG, VA., April 26, 1884.

Major Geo. N. Bliss :

DEAR SIR: I have your letter enclosing copy of my letter to you fourth of March, 1882.

I was in command of Fitz Lee's Brigade at Aldie, Va., June 17, 1863. Gen. Fitz Lee had been kicked by a mule or horse in passing a wagon, and was compelled to take an ambulance until nearly at Gettysburg. My command was composed of the 2d Va. Cavalry, my own regiment, and the 1st and 3d Va. Rosser had been sent off to the right, commanding his regiment, the 5th Va., and Wickham with the 4th Va., had been sent off, but both were sent to report to me at Aldie. The 1st, 2d and 3d Va. were feeding their horses at Carter's, about a mile and a half from Aldie, when I was notified of the advance of the enemy. Rosser arrived just before my reserve regiments got up and had a sharp skirmish. When I arrived I put the 1st Va. on the Upperville Pike, with the sharpshooters dismounted behind the two stone walls. The triangular or V shaped land between the two pikes rises to the west; at the apex was a meadow with some stocks of hay. My position was a very strong one. The enemy did not try to go up the Upperville road but once, but they charged repeatedly up the Snicker's Gap road. The sharpshooters behind the stone wall with a stake fence on their right had a splendid position. The Federals could not turn it, they would charge up the lane and receive a galling fire; my mounted regiments would counter charge and drive them back down the lane and they would get a second volley. This was done six or eight times by different squadrons and regiments, but they had not dislodged me. I never saw men show better spirit than the Federals did, and they would have run over me if two or three regiments or a brigade had been thrown in at one time. I was ordered to retire by a staff officer from Gen Stuart. I would have preferred to attempt to hold on to leaving, as my men had gained confidence and we believed we could keep them off. I did retire up the Snicker's Gap road, but was not pressed. I never saw as many dead and wounded men and horses in the same space before or after as we had before us. I do not wish at this late day to write a description of the battle. I made a report at the time, and sent in the reports of all the colonels. We captured about 130 men and officers. Rosser lost heavily. I was the ranking officer. Gen. Stuart had been held in check and kept out of Middleburg by a very inferior force compared to his command, and we never had the credit from our side for what was done by us. My command was like the R. I. regiment, fighting with five times its numbers. I believe Major McClellan, who was Gen'l Stuart's adjutant, will write a fair account of that battle in his narrative of Stuart's Campaigns now in progress.

I do not send you this as a report and do not care to appear in print, but I am responsible for the truth of what is said, and I don't care how you use it.

I hope you will excuse a hurriedly written letter and a very slight sketch of Aldie as I remember it.

Very truly yours,

THOMAS T. MUNFORD.

P. S. I was not a West Pointer. I graduated at the Virginia Military Institute, and had seventeen graduates of that school in my regiment, and I had one of the finest regiments in the army. I knew all of my men, served with them four years. I do not say this unkindly, but our army had to supply places for graduates of West Point of the old army, and some of them had better been at home.

T. T. M.

The following paper was written by Lyman Aylesworth, Sergeant of Co. C, 1st R. I. Cavalry:

MY ESCAPE FROM MIDDLEBURG.

After the charge through Middleburg I was detailed with two others to go back to the rear and picket the road we came in on. About sunset we heard the rebels charging down the road from Middleburg. When the firing commenced I rode back towards the reserve, when I saw two horses without riders coming on a regular charge. I managed to capture one of them, which was wounded in the neck; he was a very fine horse, and I think belonged to a rebel officer. Near dusk I saw a squad of about fifty cavalry coming across the field. From the direction they were our men. We challenged them to know who they were. They gave us no answer, but part of them started off to our left and part towards us. I halted them, and told them if they came any further we should fire on them. One of them said, "We are friends, I reckon." I did not want to know any more; we fired on them, and they fell back. I then had orders to draw in the picket and join the regiment. After going a short distance we met Colonel Duffié with a part of the regiment. I reported what I had seen. We then left the road and went across the field a short distance into a piece of woods and halted. We had orders in a whisper to dismount and stand by our horses ready to mount at any time. We were not allowed to build any fires or make any loud talk. As our horses had not eaten since morning it was with difficulty we could keep them still. As some of our men had lost their horses in the fight, I let a comrade have mine and took the horse I had captured, which I found to be a splendid rider. The next morning about sunrise our picket was fired on. We then mounted and moved out into the open field, where we made a charge on the enemy and drove them back. We then went into the road that led through Hopewell Gap. I was detailed with a squad of about a dozen men to cover the retreat, and I think Lieutenant Chedell had charge of the squad. We had gone only a short distance when we heard the rebels charging in our rear, and we formed across the road to meet the charge, but their force was so strong we were obliged to fall back after giving them a volley from our carbines. When we overtook the regiment the rebels were close on to us firing and yelling like madmen. We returned the fire as best we could, but the dust soon became so thick that we could hardly discern our men from the rebels. Men and horses were falling all around me. The road being very narrow, many of our-men and horses were pressed down by the crowd and trampled upon. My horse was crowded up on the bank and in coming down he stumbled and fell; I struck on my hands and feet and managed to get out of the way of the other horses by jumping over the wall into some brush. When my horse fell Lieutenant Chedell was directly in front of me, and as I was getting over the wall I saw him fall from his horse. When nearly all had passed two rebels came along and stopped. One I took to be a surgeon, and from what I could hear of their conversation, I found Lieutenant Chedell was mortally wounded. Soon after this the rebels began to march our men back as prisoners. At one time I thought I would crawl out and surrender and go with them, as my escape seemed almost impossible, but the thought of suffering and starving at Richmond or Andersonville made me decide to take the chances of escape. A number of times the rebels passed so near me that I could have touched them with my sabre, but they were all so earnestly talking of what they had captured that they did not see me. In about two hours the rebels began to fall back, and then I started for the mountains. After travelling for a short time I struck a foot-path, and soon heard voices ahead of me; thinking they were some of our men I hurried to overtake them; on coming to a short turn I saw they were three rebels, but as they were going the same way they did not discover me, and I quickly jumped into the brush and remained there until they were gone. On the way down the side of the mountain I came to a log cabin, and thinking it might be negro quarters, I went to it and found and old white man and his wife. I inquired if they had seen any Yanks pass there; they said that they had seen some that morning, who went down through the Gap. I stopped to rest, and the old lady went to the Spring House near by and brought me some milk. They said that was all they could give me as they had very little to eat. The milk, with some hard tack, I had made quite a good meal. After making some inquiry I started on. The old man informed me that if I went on in the same direction I was going I would soon be captured, but I kept on until out of his sight and then changed my course. Soon after I was discovered by some dogs, and I found a man was following me. I ordered him to halt, but he paid me no attention until I drew my revolver on him; then he stopped and inquired "if any more were coming;" I replied, "if he followed me any further he would soon find out." At Gainsville I found that some of our men had passed there that day, but no rebels. From there I took the road to Centreville, having most of the time before this travelled through the woods. Just before I reached Centreville I overtook some of our men where they had stopped for the night. Colonel Duffié saw me coming and came out to meet me. The first inquiry he made was, "Have you seen anything of Colonel Thompson?" I had not seen him, but had seen a number of our men taken prisoners. He seemed deeply affected, and said, with tears in his eyes: "My poor boys, my poor boys; All are gone. All are gone."

I had come about thirty miles and my feet were so blistered I could hardly stand on them. The next morning we went to General Hooker's headquarters.

LYMAN AYLESWORTH.

East Greenwich, R. I., January 5, 1883.

Feb. 28, 1883.

To Capt. George N. Bliss, Providence, R. I.:

DEAR SIR: You asked me at our reunion to write to you what I saw at the fight at Middleburg. I was a private in Troop H, Captain Chase's company. Soon after we left Manassas, on the morning of June 17, 1863, I was put on the skirmish line, but saw nothing of any importance until we came in sight of Thoroughfare Gap, when being then on the main road, I saw what I took to be a skirmish line on the mountain. I was then one of the advanced videttes; there were three of us, Teft, Lee, and myself, all of Company H. I then became very cautious. On the left of the Gap was a mill of some kind, and here I inquired who those men were on the hill, and received for an answer from a man through the window that he did not know. I then made up my mind that it was the enemy. Keeping a sharp lookout, with carbines ready, we moved on, and just as we almost cleared the Gap came suddenly on a Confederate, mounted, and dressed in a butternut uniform. He was about fifty feet from us. I started for him and thinking to capture him I halted him twice, but as he was turning his horse, I then took aim the best I could and fired and missed him, for away he went like a streak of lightning. This was the first shot fired. Soon after somebody on the right fired, and then commenced the skirmish at the Gap. I may say here I never saw the men go into skirmish with more spirit than they did here; they went in on the gallop and cleared the hill in a few minutes. Captain Chase came up in a short time, and I reported to him what force I thought the enemy had. I told the Captain there were six hundred of them. I saw what I estimated to be double our force take the road to the left and disappear before the regiment came up. I joined my company and was with Captain Chase when he charged into Middleburg, after which we were withdrawn to the edge of the town, and some of us were ordered to form a skirmish line by Captain Rogers, and had some lively shooting for some time. Here Captain Chase drew my attention to Sergeant Barrows, of Company E, on the left of the road alone, and exchanging shots with two or three of the enemy, (brave boy, he died at Andersonville). I went to his assistance, and was on the skirmish line until my ammunition was about gone, was then relieved and went back to the woods with the rest of the regiment. Just before sundown Captain Chase ordered us into line, and ten of us were placed under Lieutenant Steere and taken up the road a few hundred yards towards Middleburg; here we waited under a low stone wall on the right of the road. We were told that our pickets would come in ahead of the enemy, and ordered to be careful not to shoot any of our own men. About dusk we heard them coming; every one of us had his carbine and revolver ready. They came on the charge, yelling, and some of our own pickets ahead of them. Every one of the ten and our officer stood up without any protection, but the wall, which was hardly any protection whatever. On they came, and so close to us, that we could almost touch some of them with our carbines. We gave them the carbines first and then our revolvers, seventy-six shots in all. As well as I can remember, twice they charged past us to get a fire in their front, when they reached the woods. Here we stayed until another force charged, and halted about two hundred feet up the road. We could hear their officer giving them orders to form a line, and it looked like they were coming into the field where we were, and Lieutenant Steere gave us orders to follow him and we did so. I do not know how much damage was done by our seventy-six shots, but I have always believed that we helped considerable to close up the Rebellion. Our officer took us a little to the left and through the woods, and it seemed to me after going about a mile we came up with the regiment which was halted. We had all of us lost our horses, and soon after I saw a man with two, one was a captured horse; he let me have one of them, and I was again mounted. Soon after we went into the woods where we halted that night. Early in the morning we were attacked again, and in getting into the field from the woods we were very much scattered, but with the help of our Colonel and Captain Bliss and Doctor Mann, our surgeon, we soon formed a line. While we were forming, the officer in command of the enemy said to his men, "Draw your sabres and charge on them," and it was then that Captain Bliss, in a voice that would give confidence to any soldier, said, "That's just what we want," and we did not wait for them to charge, but charged them and broke them. Then we marched from the field into the road, and my place came in the middle of the column just behind the Colonel. The command took a walk, but a heavy cloud of dust towards Middleburg told us the enemy were coming and coming strong. Soon I heard firing in our rear, and an officer rode up to the Colonel and said they were firing into the rear. The Colonel turned in his saddle and took a look towards the rear, and then gave orders to take a trot, and soon it became a gallop. I had gone only a short distance, when, turning in my saddle, I saw them a few hundred yards behind, yelling, firing and ordering us to halt. Here was a scene I cannot describe; some were killed and some were thrown from their horses, and the horses without any riders kept right on with us; the road was narrow in places, and the riderless horses jumped here and there. I would sometimes look behind and they would be close to me, and they were shooting all the time. One man was killed by my side. I spoke to him when he was hit, but he never answered me. I kept on as best I could. Sometimes they would be close on me, and then I would gain some on them; after a time we were pretty well

;rung out. I passed two officers on the side of the road fixing
leir saddles. I think one of them was Captain Bixby; how they
ot away always puzzled me. Soon after I came to where two
lore of our men were fixing their saddles ; here I partly halted
nd asked them if they were going to make a stand there, but re-
aived no answer and kept on. I was all alone now, and was just
linking I would get away from them, and had just got to the end
f the wooded road on the way to the Gap, when my horse suddenly
topped. I sank my spurs into his sides, but it was no use, he was
one. I looked behind me and could see them coming, and not
aeing any possible chance, I was obliged to surrender. The first
ne took my carbine, but did not ask me for my revolver, and
nd while a dozen or more of them were gathered in a group trad-
1g for arms, and only a few feet from me, I took my revolver from
he holster and threw it over the stone wall, and none of them saw
le do it. On my way back I had the consolation that they had
ne revolver less than they might have had. Here the chase ended.
could not see that any of our men were captured beyond this
oint. On my way back the first body that I saw was that of
lieutenant Chedell. He laid with his feet towards the road, and
lthough he had been dead only a few minutes his boots were gone.
soon after I came on another of our men lying in the middle of the
oad ; he was the one to whom I spoke when he was shot. Then I
aw two more that I did not know. The next I saw was Corporal
Burton, of Company F, lying on a bank alongside of the road. As
ve passed through Middleburg I saw a number of dead Confeder-
.tes on the piazza ; how many I could not state. They were cov-
:red with sheets with bouquets placed upon their breasts.

This ends my knowledge of the fight, and I will close now with
laying that I have endeavored to give you a truthful account of it,
is far as my memory serves me, and although I may not have given

you any new facts, I have fulfilled my promise made to you at our reunion at Oakland Beach, last Summer.

Yours fraternally,

HENRY DUXBURY.

No. 3 Palmer Street, Providence, R. I.

CHICAGO, May 19, 1883.

DEAR CAPTAIN:

Your letter of last February has been allowed to remain unanswered on account of a journey which I have been taking in the South. I have suffered severely from pneumonia in the Spring in two seasons, and I thought I would try to avoid our Spring weather. The result I hope has been good. I have been quite well. I was in Florida, Southern Georgia, and the last of April in the mountains of North Carolina.

I don't know how I can assist you about your Middleburg history. Col. Duffié was sometimes communicative and sometimes, and about some matters, very reticent. I remember only in a very general way what he said to me about the affair. I know there was not the most cordial feeling between him and the controlling officers in the cavalry, and his orders to keep so far west of the main body were regarded by him as an effort to get rid of him, by having his regiment captured or lost, or by his own mistakes in executing his very difficult and very remarkable orders. You will, of course, have a copy of these, and a study of them, in view of the then known position of the main body of the Confederate army and the probable position of the cavalry, will show that there must have been some truth in Duffié's surmise. Then, again, I suspected that he was more or less a thorn in the side of the higher officers. He was not companionable with them; did not think as they did; had little in common, and, was perhaps, in clined to be boastful; perhaps solicited such a combination of regiments in brigades as would give him a larger command, and he certainly thought he was entitled to it, and felt injured that he did not receive it. Perhaps he solicited an independent command; my recollection is that he did, and when he received this, he discovered that it was sufficiently independent, and before we were through with it, we discovered that it was too much so. These jarring relations, which I have indicated in such a general way, were the cause of his being sent out. He would say that his orders were an intentional error. They would say that he asked for them and more too. He was very uneasy as soon as we were through the Bull Run Mountains, and his anxiety increased from that time on. Still he was very ambitious as well as proud, and he would not have turned back, except in the presence of an overwhelming force, for anything in the world. He sent Captain Allen dashing into (I have forgotten the name of the town) was it Middleburg, or some other at the junction of one road and the Aldie pike? and came near making splendid captures. He was exceedingly desirous of distinguishing himself, and really hoped to do so, although he knew he was liable at any moment to meet a very much larger force then he had. Still there is little distinction without danger.

I cannot tell you the secrets of his management of the affair after we had our fight, After dark, and when we knew we were in the presence of a large force, and they might surround us and overwhelm us at any moment, he was considerably shaken. He could not bear to retreat, and to stay till daylight was perhaps destruction. My recollection is that he wanted to wait before moving, until he could hear from Captain Allen's mission; but the indications of the strength of the enemy were too plain, and his final idea, I think, was to conceal his command until the morning might

5

show him a way to extricate himself. We hid successfully, but the extrication did not come. We can all say what we might have done in view of what we know now, but he was embarrassed by his relations to the cavalry officers. He could not go back to them in a disorganized state, such as would probably follow cutting through a large force in the night. He did not want to go back to them at all, and his sagacity and shrewdness was shown by the fact that he went directly to General Hooker, to whom he told such a story as induced the General to send him at once to Washington endorsed for a Brigadier-General. Duffié had no idea of returning to Pleasanton with his command gone.

Now, I have given only impressions. I have referred to no book or letters, and I may be wrong, but I think not. Duffié was in many respects an excellent soldier. His command was very fond of him, and he liked his command, but everything was subordinate to his personal ambition, and his ambition and the generally discordant relations between him and the controlling spirits of the cavalry all combined to sacrifice the regiment that day. The regiment should not have been there alone; should not have had such orders, and Duffié should have thought less of himself and more of his command and the good of the service. It demoralizes a command to skulk and hide. This was the cause of the only exception to the splendid bearing of the regiment throughout the whole expedition. The truth is, we disgraced ourselves by fleeing from a comparatively small force as we emerged from our hiding-place. A larger force came upon us later in the morning, but at first it was small. In all other respects the men acquitted themselves gallantly, and they were justified to some extent, at least, in being at first demoralized by the hiding, and the consciousness of a great danger.

I have only given you a few rambling impressions of my own and not historical facts, and have not helped you at all. I shall be very glad to see your paper, for everything relating to the history of our regiment is very interesting to me. I have within a week passed through Andersonville, Ga., and Salisbury, North Carolina. There is no appearance of a prison. Scrub pines cover the ground and have obliterated all traces of the confinement and misery of our soldiers, but the sight of the places brought up memories and accounts of experiences which will last as long as life.

I have tried to give you accurate impressions, but they are hastily written, and I should not consent to have my name mentioned as authority for anything without an opportunity for more careful expression and an examination into documents.

Very truly,

JNO. L. THOMPSON.

CAPT. GEO. N. BLISS, PROVIDENCE, R. I.

I expected to have had the revised paper to which allusion is made in the foregoing letter, but the sudden death of General Thompson, early this year, obliges me to publish this; which, in my opinion, is a graphic picture of what is sometimes called secret history. This gallant officer was, after leaving our regiment, Colonel of the First New Hampshire Cavalry, and Brevet-Brigadier General.

G. N. B.

[COPY.]

WASHINGTON, D. C., Aug. 18, 1881.

MY DEAR COMRADES OF THE 1ST N. H. CAVALRY:

Regretting greatly my inability to be present when you relight the old camp-fire, and, around its cheerful glow, fight your battles o'er, it has occurred to me that I could add something to the interest of your reunion by contributing, from the data in my possession, a paper on the affair at Middleburg, Va., in June, 1863, which ended so disastrously to our regiment (then the 1st Rhode Island), but which, in the light of history, reflects no dishonor upon us or our brave Colonel, because of the great odds of the enemy, and the perilous character of the movement required of us. Before venturing to send this paper I consulted my friend Capt. Wyatt, and was assured by him that my comrades would greet such a paper with pleasure.

While spending my summer vacation this year near Snicker's Gap, in the Blue Ridge Mountains, I took a real old cavalry ride of 36 miles one day, visiting Middleburg and Aldie. At the former place I saw the stone walls behind which our carbineers were dismounted and gallantly repulsed three charges of the "Johnnies," also the woods where the main part of the regiment was drawn up ready for a charge, while the skirmish was going on, and where subsequently Sergt. Jim Gage, of Troop K, reported to a rebel officer with his squad, supposing it was our regt. still there, and was summarily "gobbled up."

But I have already taken too much of your time with my own words. My part of this narrative will be merely the collation of reports and items, with possibly an occasional remark of my own.

My information is from official sources, with the addition of a few facts from Gen'l Robertson, of the late Confederate army, who commanded the column attacking us on the night of the 17th, and who now resides in this city, and is a very courteous and genial gentleman.

A little statement of the strength and positions of the rebel cavalry and our own may be of interest, and the accompanying rude sketch will aid in a clear understanding of the latter.

According to the regimental return of May 31, 1863, our regiment numbered 25 officers and 437 enlisted men (aggregate 462), present for duty.

(Col. Duffié calls our number 275.)

The rebel cavalry opposed to us consisted of 3 Brigades, viz. :

Robertson's, numbering 1,294 officers and men for duty ;

W. H. F. Lee's Brigade of 4 regiments, not less then 800 men ;

Fitz Hugh Lee's Brigade of 5 regiments, not less then 1,000 men.

The exact number of these two Brigades I have been unable to ascertain, though I have corresponded with their commanding officers, and examined the regimental returns. The rebel regiments, many of them, were small, but in placing them at 200 men each I am sure I have under estimated their strength.

The position of the rebel cavalry when we reached Middleburg (see sketch) was as follows:

Robertson's Brigade at Rectortown, about 8 miles; Fitz Hugh Lee's Brigade at Aldie, 5 miles; W. H. F. Lee's Brigade at White Plains, about 8 miles.

Gen'l Stuart, in person, with his staff and small pickets at Middleburg. As will be seen by Gen. Stuart's report, which follows, Robertson was present and charged us in the evening, and W. H. F. Lee engaged us the following morning. Gen'l Robertson tells me that he personally saw a part of Fitz Hugh Lee's Brigade at Middleburg on the evening of the 17th, when he attacked us, but the reports of the officers of that brigade do not mention the affair, and I presume they may not have been actively engaged, though my belief is that the portion of our regiment sent out on the Aldie road was captured by a part of this Brigade returning from that place.

In regard to the position of W. H. F. Lee's Brigade, it will be remembered that just after we passed Thoroughfare Gap we had a skirmish with a force on our left flank, in which Bill Glidden, of Company K, had his horse killed. The force here opposed to us was this brigade, and after we passed, it followed some distance in our rear.

But the report of our gallant Colonel and those of the rebel Generals R. E. Lee and J. E. B. Stuart, will best tell the story.

COL. DUFFIÉ'S REPORT.

(See Report printed in Sabres and Spurs.)

NOTE—Some errors in regard to casualties will be found in Col. Duffié's report, but these arose from the scattering condition of the regiment at the time the report was made.—TASKER.

EXTRACT FROM THE REPORT OF GEN'L R. E. LEE, CONFEDERATE STATES ARMY.

On the 17th of June, Fitz Hugh Lee's Brigade, under Col. Munford, which was on the road to Snicker's Gap, was attacked near Aldie by the Federal Cavalry. The attack was repulsed with loss, and the brigade held its ground till ordered to fall back, its right being threatened by another body coming from Hopewell towards Middleburg. The latter force was driven from Middleburg, and pursued towards Hopewell, by Robertson's Brigade, which arrived about dark. Its retreat was intercepted by W. H. Lee's Brigade, under Col. Chambliss, and the greater part of the regiment captured.

.   .   .   .   .   .

R. E. LEE,

Gen. Com. Army of N. Va.

EXTRACT FROM REPORT OF MAJ.-GEN. J. E. B STUART, COMD'G
CAVALRY DIVISION (REBEL).

.   .   .

Simultaneously with this attack (referring to the engagement at
Aldie—Tasker), I was informed that a large body of the enemy's
cavalry was advancing on Middleburg from the direction of Hopewell. Having only a few pickets and my staff here (Middleburg),
I sent word to Col. Munford (comd'g Fitz Hugh Lee's Cav. and
then at Aldie—Tasker) to look out for the road to Middleburg, as by
the time my dispatch reached him the enemy would be in the place,
and, retiring myself towards Rector's Cross Roads, I sent word
to Robertson (halted near Rectortown—Tasker) to march without
delay to Middleburg, and Chambliss (comd'g W. H. F. Lee's brigade near White Plains—Tasker) to take the Salem road to the same
place.

Brig.-Gen'l Robertson arrived at Middleburg just at dark. I
ordered him to attack the enemy at once, and with his two regts.
he drove him handsomely out of the place and pursued him ——
miles on the Hopewell road, the force appearing to scatter. He
captured a standard and 70 prisoners. Chambliss (comd'g W. H.
F. Lee's Brigade—T.), approaching from that direction, caught that
night and early next morning 160, and several guidons, the Colonel
and a small detachment, only, escaping. Horses and equipments
were captured in proportion. Among the captured were a number
of officers.

Our loss in Robertson's Brigade was slight,—3 killed and 11
wounded, except Major McNeill, 63 N. C. Cavalry, whose wound

deprived us of the services of a most valuable officer, and Lieut Col. Cantwell, 59th N. C. Cavalry, captured.

.   .   . .   .   .

Respectfully submitted,

J. E. B. STUART,

Major Gen'l Comd'g Cavalry Army of Northern Va.

From these reports will be seen the perilous nature of the movement we were ordered to undertake, the numbers, strength and positions of the opposing forces, and I think a pretty correct understanding of the whole affair can be had. Should any of the members of the old 1st R. I. have any personal recollections of this engagement I should be pleased if they would furnish them to me.

Trusting that the sketch will not prove wholly uninteresting, and wishing all my former comrades of the cavalry prosperity and happiness,

I have the honor to be your comrade and friend,

A. P. TASKER,

Late of Troop K.

www.ingramcontent.com/pod-product-compliance
Lightning Source LLC
Chambersburg PA
CBHW022040080426
42733CB00007B/908